SEP   2018

My United States

Wyoming

AUDRA WALLACE

Children's Press®
An Imprint of Scholastic Inc.

Content Consultant

James Wolfinger, PhD, Associate Dean and Professor
College of Education, DePaul University, Chicago, Illinois

Library of Congress Cataloging-in-Publication Data
Names: Wallace, Audra, author.
Title: Wyoming / by Audra Wallace.
Description: New York, NY : Children's Press, an imprint of Scholastic Inc., 2018. | Series: A true book | Includes
  bibliographical references and index.
Identifiers: LCCN 2017048742 | ISBN 9780531235867 (library binding) | ISBN 9780531250990 (pbk.)
Subjects: LCSH: Wyoming—Juvenile literature.
Classification: LCC F761.3 .W35 2018 | DDC 978.7—dc23
LC record available at https://lccn.loc.gov/2017048742

Photographs ©: cover: Quan Yuan/Getty Images; back cover: Frank Lukasseck/Getty Images; back cover ribbon: AliceLiddelle/Getty Images; 3 bottom left: Eric Nathan/Alamy Stock Photo; 3 map: Jim McMahon/Mapman ®; 4 bottom left: Jody Ann/Shutterstock; 4 center: Room's Studio/Shutterstock; 5 top: Richard Ellis/Alamy Stock Photo; 5 bottom: Digital Storm/Shutterstock; 7 center bottom: Nyker1/Dreamstime; 7 bottom: Zack Frank/Shutterstock; 7 center top: Jeff R Clow/Getty Images; 7 top: F11photo/Dreamstime; 8-9: Jeff R Clow/Getty Images; 11: Randy Beacham, All Rights Reserved; 12: National Geographic Photographer/Getty Images; 13: Jess Kraft/Shutterstock; 14: Danita Delimont/Getty Images; 15: Rob Hammer/Getty Images; 15 inset: Tom Murphy/Getty Images; 16-17: Fotosearch RM/age fotostock; 19: Inge Johnsson/Alamy Stock Photo; 20: Tigatelu/Dreamstime; 22 right: grebeshkovmaxim/Shutterstock; 22 left: cbies/Shutterstock; 23 center right: Digital Storm/Shutterstock; 23 bottom left: Jody Ann/Shutterstock; 23 top center: Room's Studio/Shutterstock; 23 center: David Stubbs/Aurora Photos; 23 bottom right: Adrianadh/Dreamstime; 23 top left: Robin Loznak/AP Images; 24-25: Wood Ronsaville Harlin Inc. USA/Bridgeman Images; 27: The Granger Collection; 29: North Wind Picture Archives/Alamy Stock Photo; 30 left: Wood Ronsaville Harlin Inc. USA/Bridgeman Images; 30 right: Zack Frank/Shutterstock; 31 bottom right: Associated Press/AP Images; 31 top right: National Park Service; 31 bottom left: Oskyle/Dreamstime; 31 top left: cbies/Shutterstock; 32: Lynn Johnson/National Geographic/Getty Images; 33: Peter Newark American Pictures/Bridgeman Images; 34-35: Richard Ellis/Alamy Stock Photo; 36: National Geographic Creative/Alamy Stock Photo; 37: Courtesy Pedigree® Stage Stop Race/Chris Havener Photographer; 38: Tomasz Tomaszewski/National Geographic Creative; 39: Robb Kendrick/National Geographic Creative/Bridgeman Images; 40 bottom right: DelightGlutenFree/Shutterstock; 40 notebook: PepitoPhotos/Getty Images; 41: Cyrus McCrimmon/Getty Images; 42 top right: GL Archive/Alamy Stock Photo; 42 bottom right: Martha Holmes/Getty Images; 42 top left: Allan Davey for Scholastic; 42 bottom left: Mary Evans Picture Library/Everett Collection; 43 center: USAF/Wikimedia; 43 bottom left: Sunset Boulevard/Getty Images; 43 top left: Michael Ochs Archives/Getty Images; 43 bottom right: Focus On Sport/Getty Images; 44 bottom: zsnavely/Stockimo/Alamy Stock Photo; 44 top: James L. Amos/Getty Images; 44 center: Eric Nathan/Alamy Stock Photo; 45 center: WEJ Scenics/Alamy Stock Photo; 45 right: Luis Castaneda/Mauritius/Superstock, Inc.; 45 left: Mark Newman/Minden Pictures; 45 bottom right: Jess Kraft/Shutterstock.

Maps by Map Hero Inc.

Scholastic Inc., 557 Broadway, New York, NY 10012

1 2 3 4 5 6 7 8 9 10 R 28 27 26 25 24 23 22 21 20 19

Front cover: Grand Prismatic Spring in Yellowstone National Park

Back cover: Cowboys on horseback

Welcome to Wyoming

Find the Truth!

UNITED STATES

Wyoming

T or F Wyoming became a state in 1776.

T or F Wyoming was the first state to grant women the right to vote.

Find the answers in this book.

Contents

THE **BIG** TRUTH!

Jade

What Represents Wyoming?

Indian paintbrush

Cheyenne Frontier Days

3 History

4 Culture

Bison

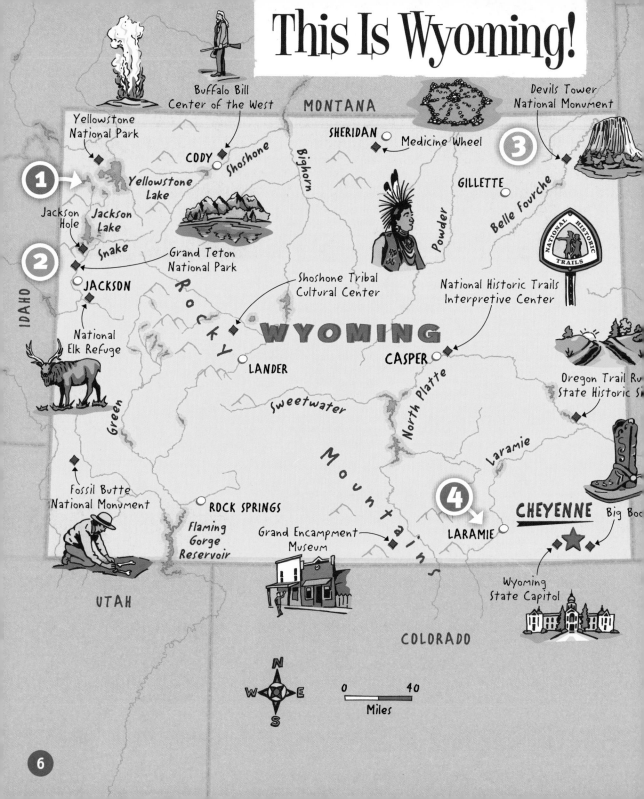

This Is Wyoming!

Buffalo Bill
Center of the West

MONTANA

Devils Tower
National Monument

Yellowstone
National Park

Medicine Wheel

SHERIDAN

③

①

CODY

Shoshone

Yellowstone
Lake

Bighorn

GILLETTE

Belle Fourche

Jackson
Hole

Jackson
Lake

Grand Teton
National Park

NATIONAL HISTORIC TRAILS

②

Snake

Rocky

Shoshone Tribal
Cultural Center

JACKSON

National
Elk Refuge

WYOMING

National Historic Trails
Interpretive Center

CASPER

Oregon Trail Ru
State Historic Si

LANDER

Sweetwater

North Platte

Green

Laramie

Fossil Butte
National Monument

Mountains

④

CHEYENNE

Big Boo

ROCK SPRINGS

Flaming
Gorge
Reservoir

Grand Encampment
Museum

LARAMIE

Wyoming
State Capitol

UTAH

COLORADO

N W E S

0   40
Miles

① Yellowstone National Park

This hot spot was the world's first national park. It's famous for its more than 10,000 active **hydrothermal** features, including a **geyser** called Old Faithful that shoots water into the sky about once every 90 minutes.

② Jackson Hole

Long ago, trappers descended steep slopes to get to this beaver-filled valley. Today, much of it is part of Grand Teton National Park.

③ Devils Tower

This enormous rock formation in northeastern Wyoming became the country's first national monument in 1906. People climb its long, vertical cracks to get to the top. It is 867 feet (264 meters) tall.

④ Fort Laramie

This national historic site was once the biggest military post in the northern plains. Now visitors can explore its many restored buildings, including a store, guardhouse, and bakery.

About 6,000 wild horses live in Wyoming.

CHAPTER 1

Land and Wildlife

Welcome to Wyoming, a symbol of the American West. Located about halfway between the Mississippi River and the Pacific Ocean, Wyoming is known for its cowboy culture and wide-open plains. Here, ranchers round up grazing cattle and sheep, while miners toil beneath the state's mineral-rich mountains. It's a place where animals roam free and the **frontier** spirit lives on.

From Mountains to Prairies

The flat, grassy Great Plains cover Wyoming's eastern half. Moving west, the land rises into the sky. Wyoming's average **elevation** is 6,700 feet (2,042 m), making it higher than any other state except Colorado. Much of this height is due to Wyoming's many snowcapped mountain ranges. These ranges are part of the Rocky Mountains.

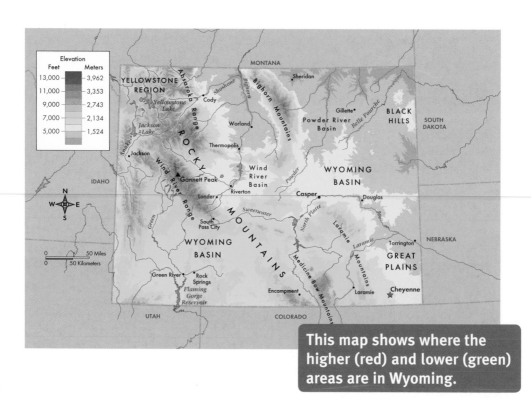

This map shows where the higher (red) and lower (green) areas are in Wyoming.

Areas such as the Red Desert of southern Wyoming receive very little rain, creating a rocky, dusty landscape.

Water from the mountains' melting snow collects in **basins** between the ranges. These bowl-like areas drain into Wyoming's many rivers and lakes. The state's main waterways are the North Platte, Snake, Green, and Yellowstone Rivers. The Great Divide Basin in south-central Wyoming doesn't drain at all. It barely gets any water. Many people enjoy sliding down the huge desert-like sand dunes there.

Cool Climate

Wyoming is sunny, cool, and dry. On average, only about 15 inches (38 centimeters) of **precipitation** fall each year. The temperature varies depending on elevation and season. It usually reaches at least 70 degrees Fahrenheit (21 degrees Celsius) in the summer. During the winter months, it drops well below freezing. Strong winds often rip through the plains. They whip the snow into blinding ground blizzards.

Bison in Grand Teton National Park rely on their thick, heavy fur to protect them from cold, snowy weather.

MAXIMUM TEMPERATURE
115°F

MINIMUM TEMPERATURE
-66°F

Famous Forests

Shoshone National Forest became the country's first national forest in 1891. National forests are areas of forest land protected by the U.S. government. Today, there are eight of them in Wyoming. The many trees that grow in these forests include Douglas firs, Engelmann spruces, and lodgepole pines. Throughout the plains, more than 100 types of grasses blanket the land. Bluegrass, wheatgrass, and tufted fescues are just a few common varieties. Cactus and sagebrush can be spotted in drier areas.

Shoshone National Forest is named for the Shoshone people, who have lived in the area for hundreds of years.

Amazing Animals

More than 100 mammals roam Wyoming's rugged landscape, including bison, elk, moose, grizzly bears, and wolves. The western part of the state is also home to the largest wintering herd of bighorn sheep in North America. Hundreds of these sheep trot atop Whiskey Mountain. In southwestern Wyoming, wild horses gallop across the wide-open plains.

A single horn from a bighorn sheep can weigh up to 30 pounds (14 kilograms).

Cutthroat trout in Yellowstone National Park

People who enjoy fishing are fond of Wyoming's lakes and streams, where fish such as cutthroat trout and bass swim. Birds such as prairie falcons, red-tailed hawks, and ospreys soar overhead. Fourteen species of snakes slither about, but only two are venomous—the prairie rattlesnake and the rare midget faded rattlesnake. The state is also home to 12 amphibian species, including the American bullfrog and the western tiger salamander.

Wyoming's state capitol was designed to look like the U.S. Capitol in Washington, D.C.

Government

The capital city of Cheyenne has been the center of Wyoming's government since the state's early days as a U.S. **territory**. It was in Cheyenne that Wyoming became the first state to give women the right to vote, serve on juries, and hold public office. This earned Wyoming its famous nickname—the Equality State. Today, Wyoming is still governed by the same constitution its leaders put in place in 1889.

Three Branches

Just like the U.S. government, Wyoming's state government is split into three branches. The governor leads the executive branch. He or she is in charge of approving **bills** and carrying out state laws. Wyoming's legislative branch creates new laws. It is made up of a Senate and a House of Representatives. The judicial branch reviews the laws and decides if they follow the state's constitution.

WYOMING'S STATE GOVERNMENT

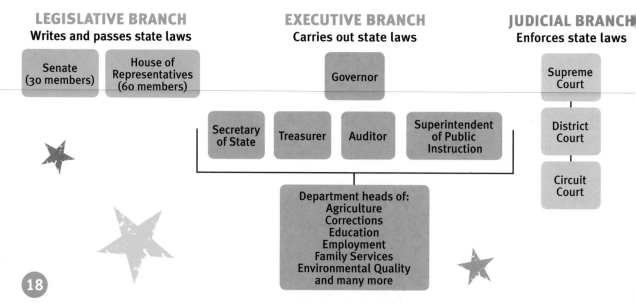

LEGISLATIVE BRANCH
Writes and passes state laws

- Senate (30 members)
- House of Representatives (60 members)

EXECUTIVE BRANCH
Carries out state laws

- Governor
  - Secretary of State
  - Treasurer
  - Auditor
  - Superintendent of Public Instruction
  - Department heads of:
    Agriculture
    Corrections
    Education
    Employment
    Family Services
    Environmental Quality
    and many more

JUDICIAL BRANCH
Enforces state laws

- Supreme Court
- District Court
- Circuit Court

The Cowboy Way

In 2010, Wyoming's legislature adopted the "Code of the West" as the state's official code of **ethics**. It is made up of 10 principles, or rules, to live by:

A cowboy on a ranch in northeastern Wyoming

- Live each day with courage.
- Take pride in your work.
- Always finish what you start.
- Do what has to be done.
- Be tough, but fair.
- When you make a promise, keep it.
- Ride for the brand. (Show loyalty and commitment to a job.)
- Talk less, say more.
- Remember that some things are not for sale.
- Know where to draw the line.

Wyoming in the National Government

Each state sends officials to represent it in the U.S. Congress. Like every state, Wyoming has two senators. The U.S. House of Representatives relies on a state's population to determine its numbers. Wyoming has one representative in the House.

Every four years, states vote on the next U.S. president. Each state is granted a number of electoral votes based on its number of members of Congress. With two senators and one representative, Wyoming has three electoral votes.

2 senators and 1 representative

3 electoral votes

Wyoming is one of seven states with only one representative in the House.

The People of Wyoming

Elected officials in Wyoming represent a population with a range of interests, lifestyles, and backgrounds.

Ethnicity (2016 estimates)

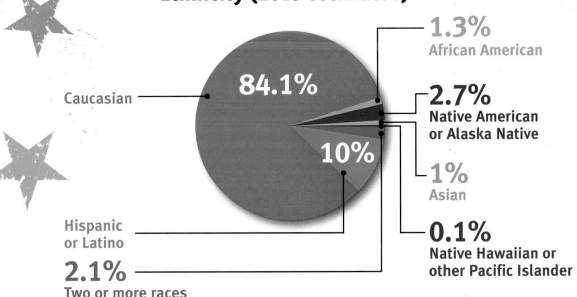

1.3%
African American

2.7%
Native American
or Alaska Native

Caucasian — **84.1%**

10%

1%
Asian

Hispanic
or Latino

0.1%
Native Hawaiian or
other Pacific Islander

2.1%
Two or more races

69.1% own their own homes.

More than **47%** live in cities with a population of 10,000 or more.

25.7% of the population have a degree beyond high school.

3.6% of Wyomingites were born in other countries.

92.3% of the population graduated high school.

48,505 Wyomingites are military veterans.

What Represents Wyoming?

States choose specific animals, plants, and objects to represent the values and characteristics of the land and its people. Find out why these symbols were chosen to represent Wyoming or discover surprising curiosities about them.

Seal

The center of the seal shows a statue of a woman holding a banner that reads "Equal Rights." This symbolizes Wyoming's history of equal rights for women. The male figures represent the state's two biggest industries—livestock and mining.

Flag

Wyoming's state flag was adopted in 1917. It shows the state seal inside the outline of a bison, the state mammal.

Western Meadowlark

STATE BIRD

This short-tailed bird features a yellow chest with a black V-shaped band across its neck.

Jade

STATE GEMSTONE

In the early 1940s, people rushed to Wyoming to look for this valuable mineral.

Bison

STATE MAMMAL

About 4,900 bison live in Yellowstone National Park.

Plains Cottonwood

STATE TREE

This fast-growing tree can get 6 feet (1.8 m) taller each year.

Indian Paintbrush

STATE FLOWER

This red-orange bloom is also known as "prairie fire."

Triceratops

STATE DINOSAUR

This giant horned dinosaur wandered Wyoming more than 65 million years ago.

The Clovis people probably wore clothing made from animal skins to protect them from cold weather.

CHAPTER 3

History

More than 12,000 years ago, humans crossed through the area now known as Wyoming for the first time. Among the prehistoric groups to visit Wyoming were the Clovis. The Clovis are famous for the stone arrowheads they left behind. These sharp weapons were made from a shiny volcanic rock found in what is now Yellowstone National Park. The Clovis used their arrows to kill mammoths, camels, and other animals that lived in the region at the time.

People of the Plains

Wyoming's name hints at its long history. It comes from the Native American phrase *mecheweami-ing*, which means "at the big plains." Many different groups of Native Americans lived in the area long before it became a state. They include the Arapaho, Cheyenne, Crow, Kiowa, and Sioux. Together, they are known as the Plains Indians. Other groups such as the Shoshone and Ute also lived in the region.

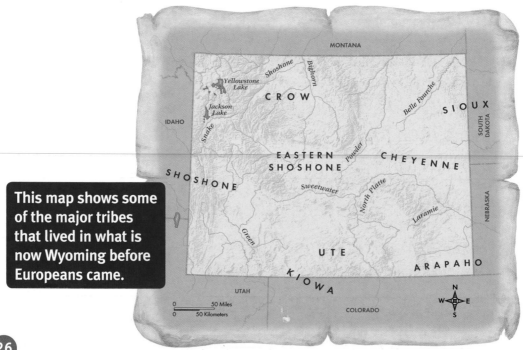

This map shows some of the major tribes that lived in what is now Wyoming before Europeans came.

A Cheyenne woman grinds wild cherries in a stone bowl in front of a tipi sometime during the 1890s.

Many of the Plains Indians were **nomadic**. They often camped in cone-shaped homes called tipis near rivers and lakes. The Plains Indians hunted herds of bison for meat. They made clothing and tools out of the bison's fur, skin, and bones. Today, only a small population of Arapaho and Shoshone remains in Wyoming. They live on the Wind River **Reservation**.

The Way West

Starting in the 1700s, various European countries, including France and Spain, claimed the land now known as Wyoming. In 1803, the United States bought some of that land from France. President Thomas Jefferson sent two explorers, Meriwether Lewis and William Clark, to map the region. John Colter, a member of the Lewis and Clark **expedition**, became one of the first known Europeans to explore Wyoming in 1807. In his journal, he wrote about Yellowstone's geysers and other natural wonders.

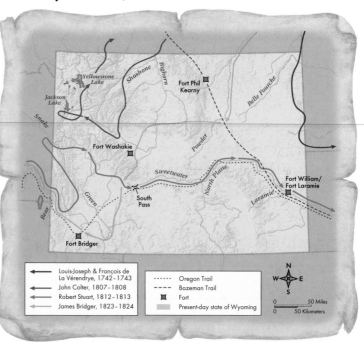

This map shows routes Europeans took as they explored and settled what is now Wyoming.

Louis-Joseph & François de La Vérendrye, 1742–1743
John Colter, 1807–1808
Robert Stuart, 1812–1813
James Bridger, 1823–1824

Oregon Trail
Bozeman Trail
Fort
Present-day state of Wyoming

0   50 Miles
0   50 Kilometers

Traders relied on horses to help them carry heavy packages of furs and other supplies across the Rocky Mountains.

Fur trappers soon followed in Lewis and Clark's footsteps. But traveling through the Rocky Mountains was difficult and dangerous. Then, in 1812, Native Americans told them about a wide valley that cut through the mountains. By the 1830s, many settlers were crossing the valley, known as South Pass, to get to Oregon, Utah, and California. In some spots, the tracks from their wagon wheels are still visible today.

All Aboard

In 1868, construction began on the first transcontinental railroad. This set the stage for one of Wyoming's biggest industries—coal mining. Coal provided fuel for the trains and jobs for new settlers. That same year, miners found small deposits of gold in Wyoming. This discovery helped prompt the U.S. government to make Wyoming an official territory.

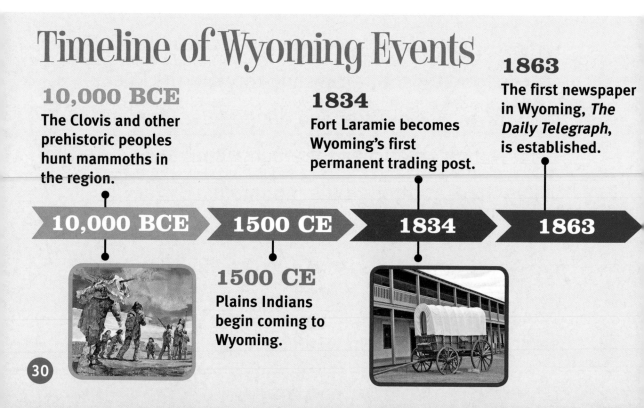

Timeline of Wyoming Events

10,000 BCE
The Clovis and other prehistoric peoples hunt mammoths in the region.

1834
Fort Laramie becomes Wyoming's first permanent trading post.

1863
The first newspaper in Wyoming, *The Daily Telegraph*, is established.

10,000 BCE	1500 CE	1834	1863

1500 CE
Plains Indians begin coming to Wyoming.

The Road to Statehood

Thousands soon journeyed to the Wyoming Territory in search of fortune and glory. They forced out many Native Americans. Cowboys and ranchers quickly moved in, and the territory's population grew to more than 60,000. Wyoming's people asked the U.S. government for statehood. On July 10, 1890, Wyoming became the 44th state.

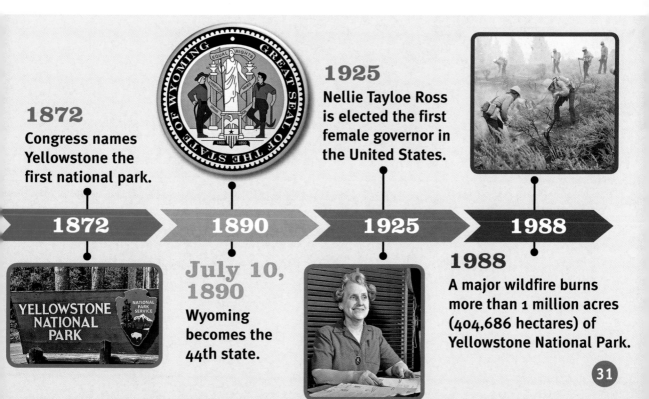

1872
Congress names Yellowstone the first national park.

1925
Nellie Tayloe Ross is elected the first female governor in the United States.

1872	1890	1925	1988

July 10, 1890
Wyoming becomes the 44th state.

1988
A major wildfire burns more than 1 million acres (404,686 hectares) of Yellowstone National Park.

YELLOWSTONE NATIONAL PARK
NATIONAL PARK SERVICE

A worker helps operate an oil drill near the town of Cody.

Modern Wyoming

Throughout the 1900s, Wyoming experienced many ups and downs. It led the nation in wool production. However, this caused many ranchers to fight over grazing land. The discovery of major oil fields kicked off a decades-long boom in production. But by the mid-1980s, the price of coal and oil had dropped. Many people left Wyoming. Today, the state's leaders are looking for ways to bring people back.

A Powerful Peacemaker

Chief Washakie is one of Wyoming's most famous leaders. During the 1860s, many Native Americans fought with the settlers who were taking over their land. As chief of the Shoshone people, Washakie worked hard to keep his people out of bloody battles. He helped negotiate peace—and the creation of the Wind River Reservation.

At the annual Cheyenne Frontier Days celebration, the Arapaho are among several Native American groups to perform traditional dances.

Culture

The Wyoming way of life is deeply tied to its cowboy roots. Herding cattle and raising sheep have played a big role in Wyoming's **economy** for more than 100 years. Even Wyoming's license plate features the image of a bucking horse and rider. Though Wyoming no longer depends on the livestock industry like it once did, rodeos and Old West festivals remain an important part of the culture.

The Cody Stampede is a popular Wyoming rodeo event that has been held every year since 1919.

Wyoming at Play

Fishing, skiing, and snowmobiling are all popular sports in Wyoming. However, no sport is more beloved than rodeo. The world's largest outdoor rodeo takes place during Frontier Days. This celebration is held each July in Cheyenne. Thousands of people chow down on chili while cowboys and cowgirls show off their skills. They rope calves, ride horses, and wrestle steers. A chuckwagon cook-off and a display of Native American traditional dancing are also part of the festivities.

Fun Things to Do

Wyoming is home to a number of annual celebrations. For example, each January, the state hosts the Pedigree Stage Stop Race, a sled dog race that starts in Jackson Hole and ends in Evanston. Over the course of a week, mushers and their dogs race hundreds of miles along a snowy course. Other fun celebrations include the Wyoming State Fair and the Plains Indian Museum Powwow.

About 5,500 dogs have participated in the Pedigree Stage Stop Race since it was first held in 1996.

Many Wyoming ranchers raise sheep for their wool, which is used to make items such as blankets and clothing.

Wyoming At Work

Wyoming's land—and what lies beneath it—drives the state's economy. Farms and ranches cover 30.3 million acres (12.3 million ha) of the state. Wyoming's deep underground **reserves** of coal, oil, and natural gas help meet the nation's energy appetite. Many people work as miners. Tourism is also a major source of jobs. Hotels, restaurants, ski resorts, and two national parks provide many employment opportunities.

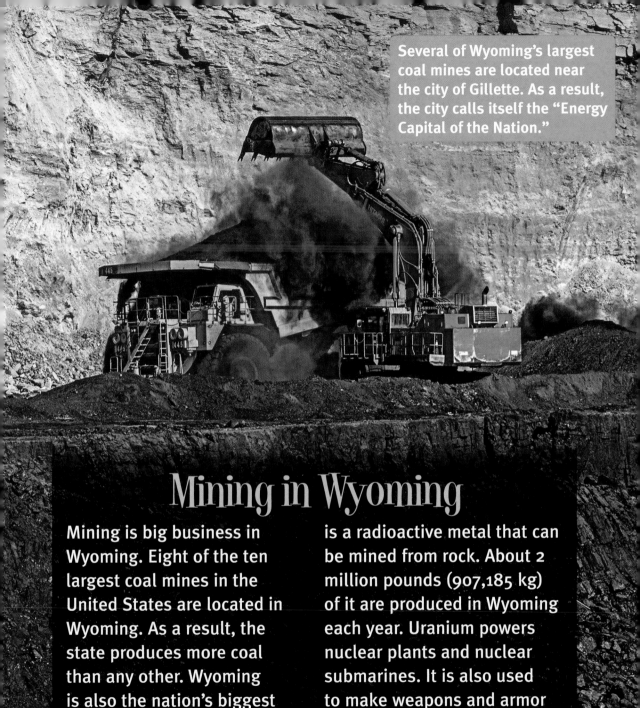

Several of Wyoming's largest coal mines are located near the city of Gillette. As a result, the city calls itself the "Energy Capital of the Nation."

Mining in Wyoming

Mining is big business in Wyoming. Eight of the ten largest coal mines in the United States are located in Wyoming. As a result, the state produces more coal than any other. Wyoming is also the nation's biggest producer of uranium. Uranium is a radioactive metal that can be mined from rock. About 2 million pounds (907,185 kg) of it are produced in Wyoming each year. Uranium powers nuclear plants and nuclear submarines. It is also used to make weapons and armor plating for tanks.

A Taste of the West

After a hard day's work, there's nothing better than a home-cooked Wyoming meal. Fresh-caught trout, elk burgers, and bison steak are among the main courses. For side dishes, many people gobble up baked beans, biscuits and gravy, and steaming bowls of chili.

Cowboy Cookies

These cookies are a popular Wyoming dessert.

Ask an adult to help you!

Ingredients

1 cup sweetened shredded coconut
$3/4$ cup chopped pecans
1 cup butter, softened
$1 \, 1/2$ cups packed brown sugar
$1/2$ cup granulated sugar
2 large eggs

$1 \, 1/2$ teaspoons vanilla extract
2 cups all-purpose flour
1 teaspoon baking soda
$1/2$ teaspoon salt
2 cups old-fashioned oats
2 cups chocolate chips

Directions

Preheat the oven to 350°F. Toast the coconut and pecans in the oven for 6 to 8 minutes. Set aside to cool. In a large bowl, mix the butter and sugars until fluffy. Add the eggs and vanilla. Mix the flour, baking soda, and salt in another bowl, then add it to the butter mixture. Beat everything together. Stir in the oats, chocolate chips, coconut, and pecans. Put teaspoon-sized balls of the mixture onto greased baking sheets. Bake for about 12 minutes. Let cool.

Like No Place on Earth

As more people discover Wyoming's wild beauty and endless skies, the population has slowly begun to grow again. Experts say it could increase by about 100,000 over the next 20 years. But no matter what the future holds for Wyoming, one thing is for sure. As one state tourism slogan proudly proclaims, Wyoming has been—and will always be—"forever west." ★

In downtown Cheyenne, giant cowboy boots painted by local artists reflect Wyoming's cowboy heritage. Each boot is about 8 feet (2.4 m) tall!

Famous People

Sacagawea

(1784–?) was a Shoshone teenager who helped the Lewis and Clark expedition communicate with Native Americans who lived in the West. She also helped guide them through parts of what is now Wyoming.

Esther Hobart Morris

(1814–1902) was the first female judge in U.S. history. She moved from Illinois to Wyoming during the gold rush. She was appointed justice of the peace on February 17, 1870.

William F. Cody

(1846–1917), also known as Buffalo Bill, was a popular sharpshooter and frontiersman. He turned his adventures into a traveling Wild West show. The city of Cody is named after him.

Jackson Pollock

(1912–1956) was a painter famous for his unique technique. Instead of using a brush, he dripped and poured paint onto huge canvases. He was born in Cody.

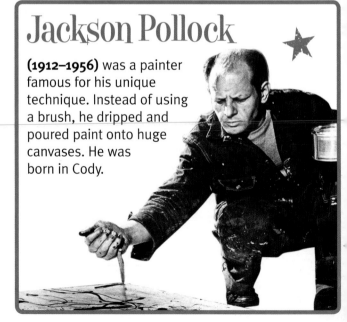

Lyle Waggoner

(1935–) is an actor who appeared in several popular TV series during the 1960s and 1970s. He lives near Jackson, where he is now a sculptor.

Dick Cheney

(1941–) served as vice president of the United States from 2001 to 2009. He spent his teenage years in Casper and later attended the University of Wyoming in Laramie.

Patricia MacLachlan

(1938–) is the author of award-winning children's books such as *Sarah, Plain and Tall*. She was born in Cheyenne.

Mike Devereaux

(1963–) is a former Major League Baseball outfielder. He started his career with the Los Angeles Dodgers and also played for the Baltimore Orioles, Chicago White Sox, Atlanta Braves, and Texas Rangers. He was born in Casper.

Harrison Ford

(1942–) is an actor best known for his roles in the *Star Wars* and *Indiana Jones* series. He owns a ranch in Jackson.

Did You Know That ...

The name of the horse on the Wyoming license plate is Old Steamboat. It first appeared on license plates in 1936. It is named after a bronco that famously could not be ridden by even the best cowboys.

Native Americans and settlers once carved or painted their names on Independence Rock as they traveled west. Some of their names can still be seen on this giant mound of granite.

The highest point in Wyoming is Gannett Peak, which is part of the Wind River Range. This giant mountain is 13,804 feet (4,207 m) tall.

The Killpecker Sand Dunes in Sweetwater County is one of seven "singing" sand dunes in the world. When sand slides down the hills, a loud hum can be heard.

The world's tallest active geyser is Steamboat Geyser in Yellowstone National Park. It can shoot water more than 300 feet (91 m) into the air.

Long ago, Native Americans once herded bison toward the edge of a deep sinkhole in Wyoming. The buffalo died, making it easy for the hunters to collect their meat and skins. Today, the pit is called the Vore Buffalo Jump. The pit's bottom contains the bones of more than 20,000 bison.

Did you find the truth?

F Wyoming became a state in 1776.

T Wyoming was the first state to grant women the right to vote.

Resources

Books

Prentzas, G. S. *Wyoming*. New York: Children's Press, 2009.

Rozett, Louise (ed.). *Fast Facts About the 50 States: Plus Puerto Rico and Washington, D.C.* New York: Children's Press, 2010.

Wallace, Audra. *Yellowstone*. New York: Children's Press, 2018.

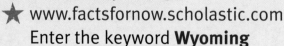

Visit this Scholastic website for more information on Wyoming:
★ www.factsfornow.scholastic.com
Enter the keyword **Wyoming**

Important Words

basins (BAY-sinz) areas of land drained by a river system

bills (BILZ) laws passed by legislators

economy (ih-KAH-nuh-mee) the system of buying, selling, making things, and managing money in a place

elevation (el-uh-VAY-shuhn) height above sea level

ethics (ETH-iks) set of principles involving what is good and bad

expedition (eks-puh-DIH-shuhn) long trip for a specific purpose

frontier (fruhn-TEER) the far edge of a country, where few people live

geyser (GYE-zur) an underground hot spring that shoots boiling water and steam into the air

hydrothermal (hye-droh-THUR-muhl) relating to hot water

nomadic (noh-MAD-ik) traveling from place to place instead of living in the same place all the time

precipitation (prih-sip-uh-TAY-shuhn) the falling of water from the sky in the form of rain, snow, hail, or sleet

reservation (rez-ur-VAY-shuhn) area of land set aside by the government for a special purpose

reserves (rih-ZURVZ) things stored or kept available for future use

territory (TER-ih-tor-ee) an area connected with or owned by a country that is outside the country's main borders

Index

Page numbers in **bold** indicate illustrations.

About the Author

Audra Wallace graduated from Ithaca College, where she studied film production and elementary education. Her passion for writing nonfiction and teaching kids led her to a position with Scholastic. Since 2006, Wallace has written and edited the award-winning classroom magazine *Scholastic News* Edition 3. She and her family enjoy exploring the great outdoors near their home in New York—and beyond!